What's that in the Ocean?

BY: MELISSA WHITTINGTON

Sting Ray

Sniffing the sea floor with its whiskery nose, This flat fishy friend wherever it goes! A hidden treasure, a graceful brown ray, The stingray glides by, waving its fins all day!

Coral

Colorful castles under the sea, Made by tiny creatures, happy and free! Coral reefs shimmer, pink, orange, and blue, A vibrant city for fishes to view!

Clown Fish

Orange stripes peek from a seaweed maze, A clownfish is playing hide-and-seek all day! Safe in its anemone, a prickly surprise, This little fish winks with bright orange eyes!

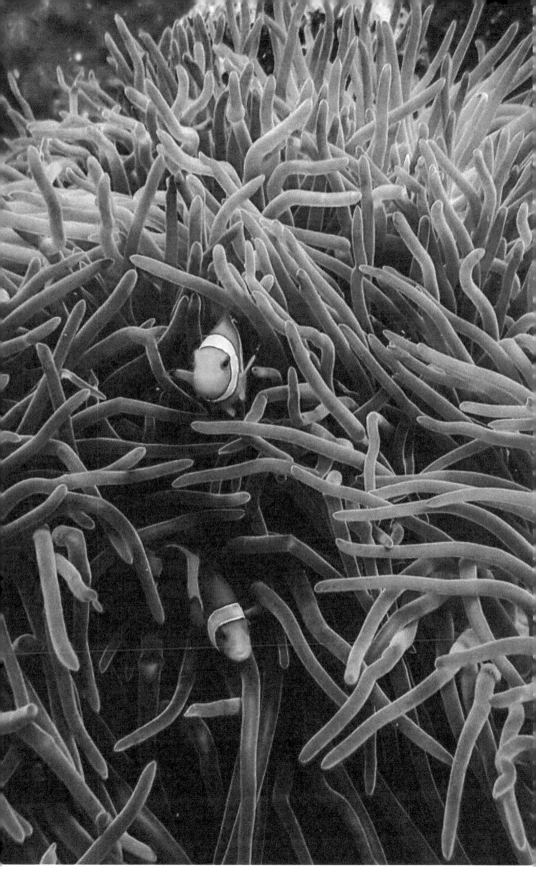

Dolphins

Clicky clicks and whistles so high, A pod of dolphins jumps to the sky! Shiny and sleek, they love to play, Flipping and splashing all through the day!

Blow Fish

Round and puffy, a
prickly surprise,
This blowfish puffs
up to double its
size! Spikes out and
grumpy, it's best to
stay far, But watch
out, it smiles when
there's no danger,
by far!

Sea Turtle

Flippers paddling, slow and wise, A sea turtle travels beneath the skies. A shell on its back, a treasure to hold, It swims the big oceans, brave and bold!

Sea Anemone

A crown of tentacles, swaying so slow, The sea anemone whispers, "Hey there, little fellow!" Hiding inside, a clownfish so bright, They share a snug home, a colorful sight!

Sharks

Fin like a triangle, teeth in a grin, The ocean keeps healthy with this mighty fin! Sharks keep things balanced, a ruler of sorts, They chase after fishies of all shapes and sorts!

Sea Horse

Tail curled tight, a funny little steed, The seahorse holds on with all its might! Dads take care of the eggs, a sight to behold, These underwater riders are strong and bold!

School

Shimmering scales,
a flash of delight, A
school of fish swims,
a dazzling sight!
Silver and blue,
they swirl and they
dart, Following the
leader, playing their
part!

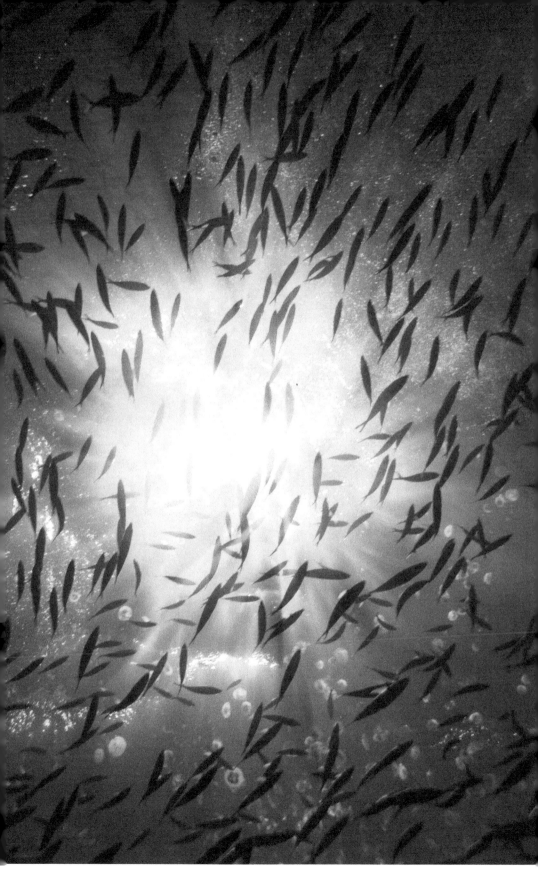

Octopus

Eight wiggly arms, a
curious face, The
octopus peeks from
its hiding place!
Squirting black ink, a
magic trick neat,
This clever sea
friend can't be beat!

Jellyfish

Like a floating umbrella, all blobby and blue, The jellyfish glides, with tentacles too! Don't touch its streamers, they might give a sting, But watch from afar, this graceful sea thing!

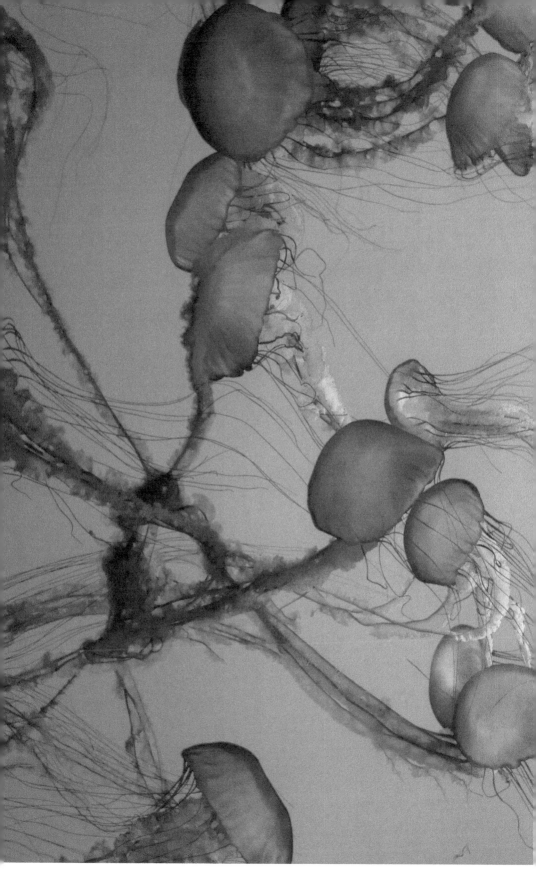

Scuba Diver

Bubbles all around, a
helmet so bright, A
scuba diver explores
with all their might!
Goggles on tight,
with fins for a kick,
They visit the ocean,
a magical trick!

Eel

Slithery and sleek, a wiggle and a coil, The eel winds its way, a fishy, long foil! Hiding in rocks, it's a mystery to find, This slippery swimmer leaves most fish behind!

Walrus

Big tusks and a mustache, a blubbery friend, The walrus loves lounging on the icy trend! Clams are its favorite, they slurp with delight, These funny fellows waddle with all their might!

Starfish

Five pointed arms
reaching for the sun,
A starfish sparkles,
oh what fun! But
hold on tight, don't
take it away,
Starfish need water
to live and play!

Sea Urchin

Spikes all around, a prickly ball, The sea urchin munches on seaweed so tall! Don't step on its back, it might give you a poke, But under its spines, a hidden world to explore!

Whales

Biggest singers in
the ocean so deep,
Whales sing loud
songs that make
fishes leap! Spouting
tall fountains, a
watery surprise,
These gentle giants
swim beneath the
skies!

Angel Fish

Fins like flowing ribbons, shimmering bright, The angelfish glides, a dazzling sight! With stripes of orange, blue, and yellow too, It swims through the coral, a graceful view!

Good
Bye

Printed in the USA
CPSIA information can be obtained
at www.ICGtesting.com
LVHW020301091024
793327LV00001B/20